TABLE OF CONTENTS

01 — BREAKFAST & BREADS

Vegan Granola
Garlic Rosemary Home Fries
Mung Bean Quiche with Lime
Blueberry Breakfast Cobbler
Potato Flautas with Green Chili Sauce
Strawberry Breakfast Parfait
Banana Chia Bread
Cheesy Breakfast Sandwich
French Toast
Corn Ribs

02 — SIDES & SNACKS

Garlic Lime Tortilla Chips
Indian Spiced Okra
Simple Roasted Zucchini
Air Fried Vegan Pakoras
Baked Potato
Air Fried Pita Chips
Two Ways Carrots
Air Fried Green Tomatoes
Cheesy French Fries with Shallots
Air Fried Cabbage

MAIN DISHES

03

Homemade Air Fried Veggie Burgers
Vegan Cauliflower Buffalo Wings
Spaghetti Squash
Air Fried Mushrooms
Panang Curry Bowl
Red Curry Noodles w. Sesame Crunch Tofu
Eggplant Parmigiana
BBQ Jackfruit Nachos
Ginger Tahini Noodles w. Sesame Crunch Tofu
Cauliflower Steak

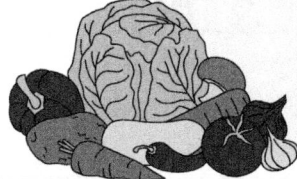

DESSERTS

Pineapple Upside-Down Cake
Air Fried Strawberries
Vegan Lemon Bars
Chocolate Chip Cookies
Oatmeal Raisin Cookies
Vegan Chocolate Cake
Air Fried Bananas
Baked Apples
Air Fried Peaches
Apple Puffs with Vanilla Caramel Sauce

04

STAPLES

05

Non Dairy Ranch Dressing
Asian Spicy Sweet Sauce
Cheesy Sauce
Vegan BBQ Sauce
Cilantro Chutney
Crisp Tofu
Sesame Crunch Tofu
Green Chili Sauce

1
Breakfast & Breads

Vegan Granola

FAMILY-FRIENDLY

SERVING	PREP TIME	COOK TIME	BAKE
4	5 mins	40 mins	248°F

INGREDIENTS

- **1 cup rolled oats**
- **3 tablespoons maple syrup**
- **1 tablespoon coconut sugar**
- **1 tablespoon neutral-flavored oil (such as refined coconut, sunflower, or safflower)**
- **¼ teaspoon sea salt**
- **¼ teaspoon cinnamon**
- **¼ teaspoon vanilla**

INSTRUCTIONS

1. **In** a medium mixing bowl, combine the oats, maple syrup, coconut sugar, oil, salt, cinnamon, and vanilla until well blended. Place in a 6-inch circular, 2-inch-deep baking sheet and bake for 10 minutes.
2. **Remove**, stir well, and cook for a further 10 minutes. Repeat this process for a total of 40 minutes, or until the granola is lightly toasted and mostly dry. It will not be completely crisp yet, but it will become crisp after being placed to a platter and allowed to cool.
3. **Once** fully cold and crisp, store in an airtight container. The granola should last for a week or two in a cold, dry area.

Per Serving: Calories: 165; Total fat: 5g; Saturated fat: 1g; Cholesterol: 0mg; Sodium: 120mg; Carbohydrates: 27g; Fiber: 2g; Protein: 3g

Garlic Rosemary Home Fries

FAST / FAMILY-FRIENDLY / GLUTEN-FREE

SERVING	PREP TIME	COOK TIME	ROAST
4	5 mins	16 mins	392°F

INGREDIENTS

- **2 cups cubed potato (small cubes from 2 medium potatoes)**
- **1½ teaspoons oil (olive or sunflower)**
- **3 medium cloves garlic, minced or pressed**
- **¼ teaspoon sea salt**
- **¼ teaspoon onion granules**
- **⅛ teaspoon freshly ground black pepper**
- **Cooking oil spray (sunflower, safflower, or refined coconut)**
- **½ tablespoon dried rosemary or fresh rosemary, minced**

INSTRUCTIONS

1. **In** a medium bowl, combine the potatoes, oil, garlic, salt, onion granules, and black pepper. Stir in the seasonings until the potatoes are evenly coated. Put the potato mixture in the air fryer basket and roast for 8 minutes. Set the bowl aside.
2. **Remove**, shake the basket, or toss the contents, and cook for a further 8 minutes, or until the potatoes are soft and well-browned. Return the potatoes to the bowl and sprinkle with oil. Toss in the rosemary and serve immediately.

Tips:
- You may make this dish more interesting by trying out several versions. To make an Indian-inspired version, substitute the rosemary with turmeric, coriander, cumin, and cayenne. Alternatively, prepare a smokey Mexican-style version with chipotle, lime, and cumin (without the rosemary).

Per Serving: Calories: 103; Total fat: 2g; Saturated fat: 0g; Cholesterol: 0mg; Sodium: 124mg; Carbohydrates: 20g; Fiber: 3g; Protein: 2g

Mung Bean Quiche with Lime

GLUTEN-FREE

SERVING	PREP TIME	COOK TIME	BAKE
2	5 mins (plus overnight soaking)	15 mins	392°F

INGREDIENTS

- **2 teaspoons tamari or shoyu**
- **1 teaspoon fresh lime juice**
- **1 large garlic clove, minced or pressed**
- **Dash red chili flakes**
- **½ cup mung beans**
- **½ cup water**
- **¼ teaspoon sea salt**
- **⅛ teaspoon freshly ground black pepper**
- **½ cup minced onion**
- **1 scallion, trimmed and chopped**
- **Cooking oil spray (sunflower, safflower, or refined coconut)**

INSTRUCTIONS

1. **In** a small bowl, combine the tamari, lime juice, garlic, and chili flakes. Set aside. This can be done while the tofu is cooking, or the night before. If you choose the latter, simply store in an airtight container in the refrigerator.
2. **Soak** the mung beans in plenty of water overnight, or for approximately 8 hours. Drain and rinse the mung beans, then set aside.
3. **Preheat** the air fryer for 2 minutes, then insert the 6-inch round, 2-inch deep baking pan.
4. **In** a blender, combine the soaked and drained beans, water, salt, and pepper. Blend until smooth. Stir in the onion and scallions, but don't mix.
5. **Spray** the prepared pan with oil spray, then pour in the batter. Bake 15 minutes, or until golden brown. Once cooked, cut the "quiche" into quarters and drizzle with the sauce.

Tips:
- If you want a more robust flavor, add a small amount of neutral-flavored oil to the batter—or coat the baking pan with more oil.

Per Serving: Calories: 204; Total fat: 1g; Saturated fat: 0g; Cholesterol: 0mg; Sodium: 580mg; Carbohydrates: 38g; Fiber: 9g; Protein: 14g

Blueberry Breakfast Cobbler

FAST / FAMILY-FRIENDLY

SERVING	PREP TIME	COOK TIME	BAKE
4	5 mins	15 mins	347°F

INGREDIENTS

- ⅓ cup whole-wheat pastry flour
- ¾ teaspoon baking powder
- Dash sea salt
- ⅓ cup unsweetened nondairy milk
- 2 tablespoons maple syrup
- ½ teaspoon vanilla
- Cooking oil spray (sunflower, safflower, or refined coconut)
- ½ cup blueberries
- ¼ cup granola, plain, or Vegan Granola
- Nondairy yogurt (for topping, optional)

INSTRUCTIONS

1. **In** a larger bowl, combine the flour, baking powder, and salt. Add the milk, maple syrup, and vanilla, whisking gently until just blended.
2. **Spray** a 6-inch round, 2-inch deep baking pan with cooking oil, then pour the mixture into it with a rubber spatula to ensure that no goodness is lost. Sprinkle the blueberries and granola evenly over top.
3. **Place** the pan in the air fryer and bake for 15 minutes, or until well browned and a knife inserted in the center comes out clean (except for the sticky blueberries). Enjoy plain or with a small dollop of nondairy vanilla yogurt.

Per Serving: Calories: 144; Total fat: 4g; Saturated fat: 1g; Cholesterol: 0mg; Sodium: 29mg; Carbohydrates: 24g; Fiber: 3g; Protein: 3g

Potato Flautas with Green Chili Sauce

FAST / FAMILY-FRIENDLY / GLUTEN-FREE

SERVING	PREP TIME	COOK TIME	FRY
2 (makes 4 flautas)	20 mins	8 mins	392°F

INGREDIENTS

- 1 medium potato, peeled and chopped into small cubes (1½ cups chopped potato)
- 2 tablespoons nondairy milk, plain and unsweetened
- 2 large garlic cloves, minced or pressed
- ¼ teaspoon sea salt
- ⅛ teaspoon freshly ground black pepper
- 2 tablespoons minced scallions
- 4 sprouted corn tortillas
- Cooking oil spray (sunflower, safflower, or refined coconut)
- **Green Chili Sauce or fresh salsa**
- **Guacamole or fresh avocado slices (optional)**
- **Cilantro, minced (optional)**

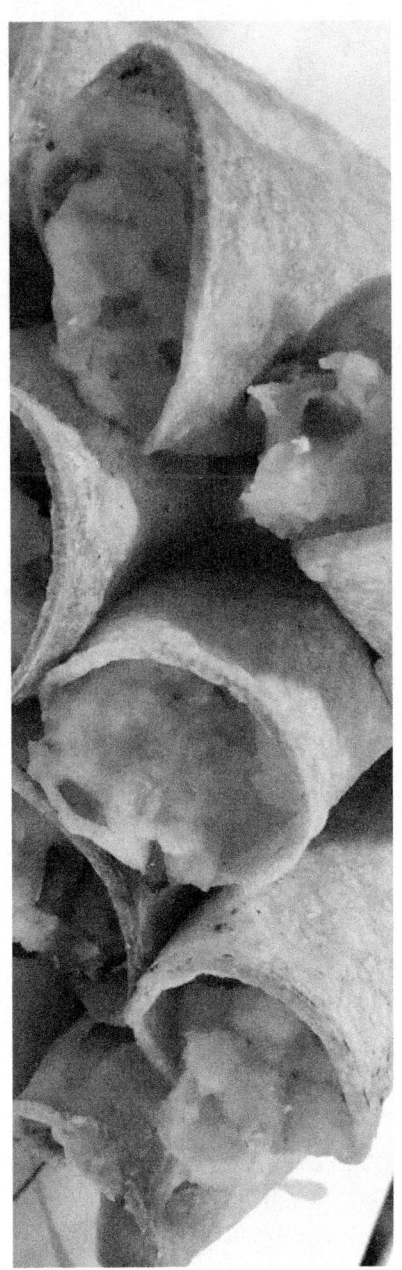

INSTRUCTIONS

1. **Cook** the potato cubes in a pot on the stovetop with a steamer basket for 15 minutes, or until cooked. While they are steaming, you will have enough time to prepare the Green Chili Sauce, if using.
2. **Place** the cooked potato cubes in a bowl and mash with a fork or potato masher. Add the milk, garlic, salt, and pepper, and mix thoroughly. Add the scallions and whisk into the mixture. Set the bowl aside.
3. **Warm** the tortillas (to prevent them from breaking): Run them under water for a second, then set them in an oil-sprayed air fryer basket (you can stack them). Fry for one minute.
4. **Transfer** the tortillas to a flat surface, arranging them individually. Spread an equal quantity of potato filling in the center of each tortilla. Roll the tortilla sides up over the filling and set seam side down in the air fryer basket (this keeps the tortillas from flying apart). Spray the tops with oil. Fry the tortillas for 7 minutes, or until golden brown and faintly crisp. Serve with sauce or salsa, and any additional toppings as desired.

Per Serving: Calories: 218; Total fat: 2g; Saturated fat: 0g; Cholesterol: 0mg; Sodium: 324mg; Carbohydrates: 46g; Fiber: 7g; Protein: 6g

Strawberry Breakfast Parfait

FAMILY-FRIENDLY

SERVING	PREP TIME	COOK TIME	BAKE
4	10 mins (includes granola cooking time)	40 mins	248°F

INGREDIENTS

- **Vegan Granola**
- **1 (12.3-ounce) package silken tofu, firm or extra-firm**
- **2 pitted dates (optional)**
- **¼ cup maple syrup**
- **1 cup strawberries (fresh or frozen), plus 3 cups fresh strawberries, sliced**
- **2 tablespoons neutral-flavored oil (such as refined coconut, sunflower, or safflower)**
- **2 teaspoons vanilla**
- **⅛ teaspoon sea salt**

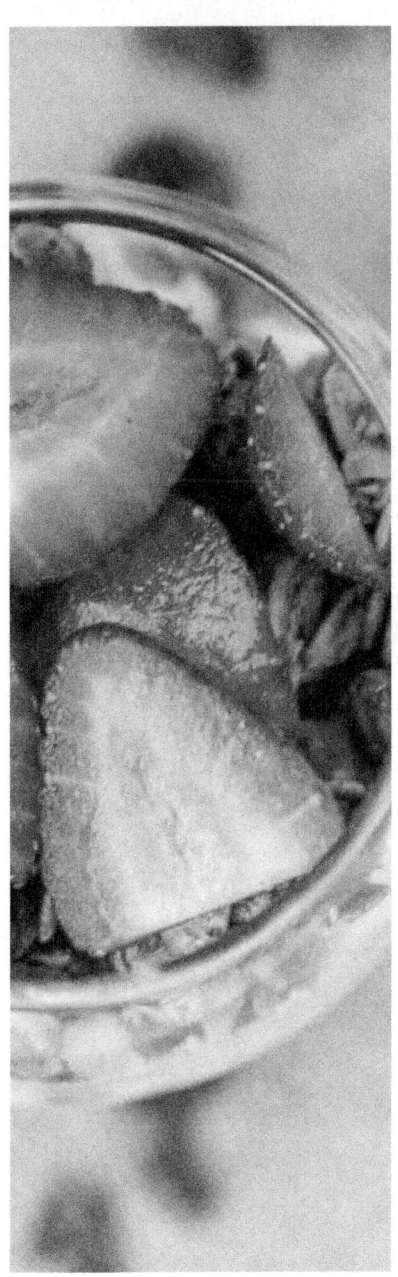

INSTRUCTIONS

1. **Prepare** the granola and set aside. While you're doing that, you can prepare the remaining items.
2. **In** a blender, combine the tofu, dates (if using), and maple syrup. Blend until smooth. Blend in 1 cup of strawberries, oil, vanilla, and salt until velvety smooth. Set away (this component will keep refrigerated in an airtight jar for about a week).
3. **Layer** the parfaits. Gather some clear glasses or parfait cups—the prettier, the better. Place granola on the bottom, cover with the strawberry cream, then sprinkle with the sliced fresh strawberries. Repeat until you have the appropriate number of layers. Enjoy immediately to maintain the crunch of the granola.

Tips:
- If you don't have a high-speed blender (Vitamix or Blendtec), soak the optional dates in water for an hour or two until they are soft enough to blend smoothly. If so, drain the water after steeping to ensure that the cream is creamy rather than watery.

Per Serving: Calories: 377; Total fat: 14g; Saturated fat: 2g; Cholesterol: 0mg; Sodium: 335mg; Carbohydrates: 53g; Fiber: 5g; Protein: 10g

Banana Chia Bread

FAMILY-FRIENDLY

SERVING	PREP TIME	COOK TIME	BAKE
6	10 mins	25 mins	347°F

INGREDIENTS

- 2 large bananas, very ripe, peeled (1 cup mashed banana)
- 2 tablespoons neutral-flavored oil (sunflower or safflower)
- 2 tablespoons maple syrup
- ½ teaspoon vanilla
- ½ tablespoon chia seeds
- ½ tablespoon ground flaxseed
- 1 cup whole-wheat pastry flour
- ¼ cup coconut sugar
- ½ teaspoon cinnamon
- ¼ teaspoon salt
- ¼ teaspoon nutmeg
- ¼ teaspoon baking powder
- ¼ teaspoon baking soda
- Cooking oil spray (sunflower, safflower, or refined coconut)

INSTRUCTIONS

1. **In** a medium mixing bowl, mash the peeled bananas with a fork until very mushy. Stir in the oil, maple syrup, vanilla, chia, and flaxseeds until thoroughly combined.
2. **Add** the flour, sugar, cinnamon, salt, nutmeg, baking powder, and baking soda; whisk just until incorporated.
3. **Preheat** an air fryer for 2 minutes. Use a 6-inch round, 2-inch deep baking pan.
4. **Open** the basket, brush the baking pan with oil, and pour the batter in. Smooth the top with a rubber spatula before baking for 25 minutes.
5. **Remove** and cool for a minute or two before cutting into wedges and serving.

Tips:
- An extra-ripe banana is great for this bread, as well as smoothies and shakes, because it adds natural fruit sweetness without the need for added sugar.

Per Serving: Calories: 202; Total fat: 6g; Saturated fat: 1g; Cholesterol: 0mg; Sodium: 151mg; Carbohydrates: 36g; Fiber: 4g; Protein: 3g

Cheesy Breakfast Sandwich

FAST / FAMILY-FRIENDLY

SERVING	PREP TIME	COOK TIME	BAKE
2	15 mins (including Cheesy Sauce)	13 mins	392°F

INGREDIENTS

- 1 (8-ounce) package firm or extra-firm tofu, thinly sliced into rectangles or squares
- 2 teaspoons nutritional yeast, divided
- ¼ teaspoon sea salt, divided
- ⅛ teaspoon freshly ground black pepper, divided
- Cooking oil spray (sunflower, safflower, or refined coconut)
- 4 slices bread
- Vegan tempeh bacon (optional)
- Vegan mayo, your choice (optional)
- Leaf lettuce, dill pickles, and thinly sliced red onion (optional)

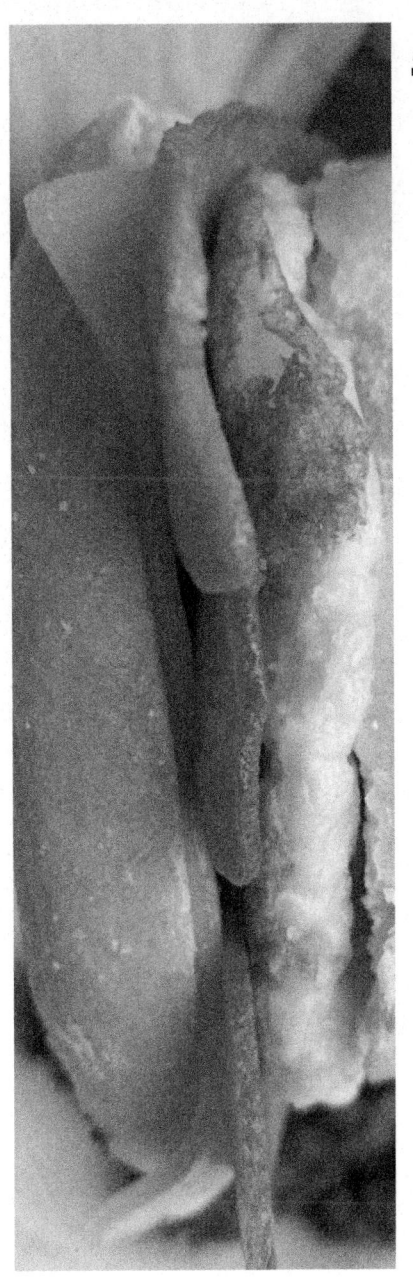

INSTRUCTIONS

1. **Spread** the tofu slices in a single layer on a platter and season with 1 teaspoon nutritional yeast, 1/8 teaspoon salt, and 1/16 teaspoon pepper. Turn over and sprinkle the remaining yeast, salt, and pepper over the top.
2. **Spray** the air fryer basket with oil, then arrange the tofu pieces in a single layer. Spray oil on the tops. Bake for seven minutes.
3. **While** the tofu cooks, prepare your optional toppings.
4. **After** 7 minutes, turn the tofu and coat with oil again. Bake for another 6 minutes, or until golden and slightly crisp.
5. **Toast** the toast, then top with the tofu slices, Cheesy Sauce, vegan meat (if using), and any other desired toppings. Devour instantly.

Per Serving: Calories: 199; Total fat: 8g; Saturated fat: 1g; Cholesterol: 0mg; Sodium: 522mg; Carbohydrates: 21g; Fiber: 6g; Protein: 15g

French Toast

FAST / FAMILY-FRIENDLY

SERVING: 3
PREP TIME: 8 mins
COOK TIME: 10 mins
FRY: 370°F

INGREDIENTS

- 5 or 6 slices vegan brioche or other thick sandwich bread
- 1 ¼ cups plain unsweetened soy milk - or your favorite plant milk such as oat, coconut, or almond milk
- ¼ cup corn starch
- 2 tablespoons maple syrup
- 2 teaspoons vanilla extract
- 1 rounded teaspoon ground cinnamon
- ⅛ teaspoon ground nutmeg
- ⅛ teaspoon fine sea salt
- Vegan butter, maple syrup, fresh berries

INSTRUCTIONS

1. **Preheat** the air fryer to 370 degrees F. In a large shallow bowl or other dish, whisk together the ingredients for the batter.
2. **Soak** each slice of bread for about 30 seconds per side or until saturated. Once the air fryer is preheated, lightly spray the cooking surface with oil.
3. **As** you pick up the pieces of bread from the liquid, let the excess drain back into the dish. Arrange the bread in a single layer in the air fryer. Cook for 10 minutes, flipping after 5 to 6 minutes. NOTE: this cook time is for thick vegan brioche; thinner pieces of bread will cook more quickly.
4. **French** toast is done when both sides are browned and crisp, and the interior is hot and custardy. Serve warm with desired toppings.

Storing Tips: French toast is best served fresh. Leftovers can be kept in the fridge for up to four days or frozen for up to two months. Reheat in an air fryer, oven, or skillet on the stove.

Per Serving: Calories: 430kcal; Carbohydrates: 70g; Protein: 11g; Fat: 10g; Fiber: 3g; Sugar: 20g

Vegan Corn Ribs

FAST / FAMILY-FRIENDLY / GLUTEN-FREE

SERVING	PREP TIME	COOK TIME	FRY
4	10 mins	10 mins	380°F

INGREDIENTS

- **2 corn on the cob**
- **3-4 tablespoons Vegan BBQ Sauce**

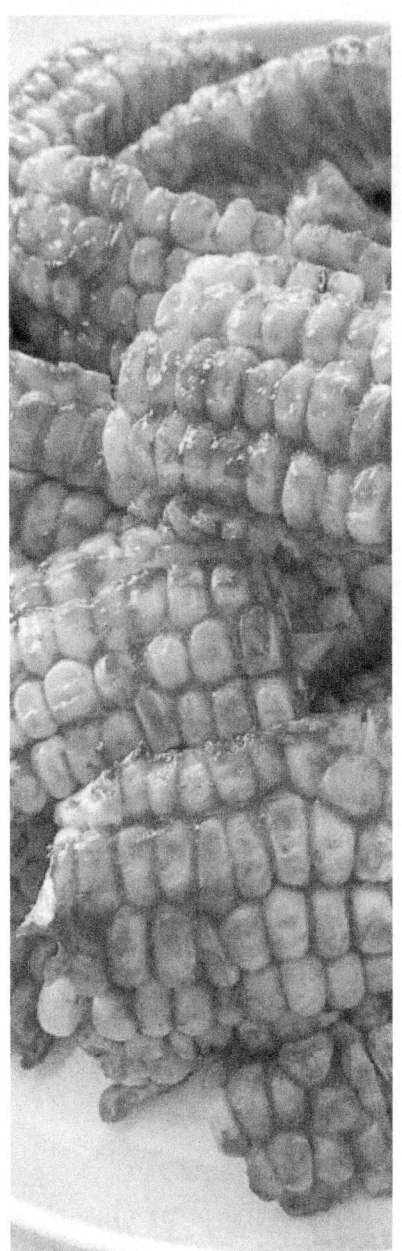

INSTRUCTIONS

1. **Remove** the husk and use a sharp knife to cut each corn in half to make them easier to quarter. Then stand each piece upright (the flat side that you just cut down on the cutting board for stability) and slice in half vertically. Then place those pieces core side down and cut in half again. You will end up with 8 corn ribs from each corn on the cob for 16 pieces in total. The goal is to not squish the kernels so this cutting method works best.
2. **Brush** each corn rib with Vegan BBQ Sauce and place them in the basket of your fryer in an even layer. It's okay if they are overlapping a little. Air fry at 380°F/193°C for 10-12 minutes and enjoy.

Tips:
- Choose corn that is fresh, with thicker kernels. The husks should be tightly wrapped, bright green, and not turning yellow or dry.
- Use extreme caution when cutting your corn into "ribs".

Per Serving: Calories: 51cal; Carbohydrates: 11g; Protein: 1g; Fat: 1g; Sodium: 169mg; Potassium: 133mg; Fiber: 1g; Sugar: 5g; Calcium: 4mg

Air Fry Revolution – Get Crispy Without the Guilt

2
Sides & Snacks

Garlic Lime Tortilla Chips

FAST / FAMILY-FRIENDLY / GLUTEN-FREE

SERVING	PREP TIME	COOK TIME	FRY
3	2 mins	7 mins	347°F

INGREDIENTS

- **4 corn tortillas**
- **½ teaspoon garlic granules**
- **⅛ to ¼ teaspoon sea salt**
- **2½ teaspoons fresh lime juice**
- **Cooking oil spray (coconut, sunflower, or safflower)**

INSTRUCTIONS

1. **Cut** the tortillas in quarters. Place in a medium bowl and gently toss with the garlic, salt, and lime juice.
2. **Spray** the air fryer basket with oil, then add the chips and cook for 3 minutes. Remove the air fryer basket, toss (to ensure that the chips cook evenly), and spray again with oil. Fry for another two minutes. Remove one last time, toss, spray with oil, and cook for 2 minutes, or until golden brown and crisp. These may not all cook at the same rate, so keep an eye out for the ones that are done. Allow it sit at room temperature for a few minutes to crisp up before enjoying.

Per Serving: Calories: 73; Total fat: 1g; Saturated fat: 0g; Cholesterol: 0mg; Sodium: 93mg; Carbohydrates: 15g; Fiber: 2g; Protein: 2g

Indian Spiced Okra

FAST / GLUTEN-FREE

SERVING	PREP TIME	COOK TIME	FRY
4	5 mins	20 mins	392°F

INGREDIENTS

- ½ pound okra (3 cups)
- 1 tablespoon coconut oil, melted
- 1 teaspoon cumin
- 1 teaspoon coriander
- 1 teaspoon garlic granules
- ¼ teaspoon sea salt
- ¼ teaspoon turmeric
- ⅛ teaspoon cayenne
- 1 teaspoon fresh lime juice

INSTRUCTIONS

1. **Place** the okra in a medium basin and stir with the oil. Combine cumin, coriander, garlic, salt, turmeric, and cayenne. Stir well, preferably with a rubber spatula, until the okra is thoroughly coated with the seasonings.
2. **Place** the okra in an air fryer basket and cook for 7 minutes. Set the seasoning bowl aside. Remove the air fryer basket, stir or toss the okra to ensure it is evenly cooked, then return it to the air fryer for another 7 minutes. Remove the basket, toss it, and check for doneness. At this time, your okra will most likely need to be fried for another 6 minutes, depending on its size (smaller pieces cook faster). Remove when the pieces feel crisp, not "squishy."
3. **Once** the okra is crisp, return it to the seasoning bowl. Sprinkle the lime juice on top, give the okra a final swirl, and serve immediately.

Per Serving: Calories: 58; Total fat: 4g; Saturated fat: 3g; Cholesterol: 0mg; Sodium: 123mg; Carbohydrates: 6g; Fiber: 2g; Protein: 1g

Simple Roasted Zucchini

FAST / FAMILY-FRIENDLY / GLUTEN-FREE

SERVING	PREP TIME	COOK TIME	ROAST
4	2 mins	14 mins	392°F

INGREDIENTS

- Cooking oil spray (sunflower, safflower, or refined coconut)
- 2 zucchini, sliced in ¼- to ½-inch-thick rounds (about 2 cups)
- ¼ teaspoon garlic granules
- ⅛ teaspoon sea salt
- Freshly ground black pepper (optional)

INSTRUCTIONS

1. **Spray** the air fryer basket with oil. Place the zucchini rounds in the basket, spreading them out as much as possible. Sprinkle the garlic, salt, and pepper over the tops, if using. Spray with oil, then roast for 7 minutes.
2. **Remove** the basket from the air fryer, toss or flip the zucchini with a spatula to ensure consistent cooking, and spritz again with oil. Roast for an additional 7 minutes, or until the zucchini rounds are well browned and soft.

Per Serving: Calories: 17; Total fat: 0g; Saturated fat: 0g; Cholesterol: 0mg; Sodium: 68mg; Carbohydrates: 3g; Fiber: 1g; Protein: 1g

Air Fried Vegan Pakoras

FAST / FAMILY-FRIENDLY / GLUTEN-FREE

SERVING 5 (makes 20 pakoras) | PREP TIME 10 mins | COOK TIME 16 mins | FRY 347°F

INGREDIENTS

- ⅔ cup chickpea flour
- 1 tablespoon arrowroot (or cornstarch)
- 1½ teaspoons sea salt
- 2 teaspoons cumin powder
- ½ teaspoon coriander powder
- ½ teaspoon turmeric
- ⅛ teaspoon baking soda
- ⅛ teaspoon cayenne powder
- 1½ cups minced onion
- ½ cup chopped cilantro
- ½ cup finely chopped cauliflower
- ¼ cup fresh lemon juice
- Cooking oil spray (coconut, sunflower, or safflower)

INSTRUCTIONS

1. **In** a medium mixing bowl, combine the chickpea flour, arrowroot, salt, cumin, coriander, turmeric, baking soda, and cayenne. Stir thoroughly.
2. **Combine** the onion, cilantro, cauliflower, and lemon juice with the flour mixture. Stir thoroughly. Set aside.
3. **Spray** the air fryer basket with oil and set it aside. Take a plate and set it aside as well.
4. **Use** your hands to stir the mixture again, kneading the flour and spices into the vegetables. Take small pieces (approximately 1 tablespoon—so they cook all the way through) and smash them together with your palm to form a 1-inch ball. Place in an air fryer.
5. **Repeat** with the remaining batter, creating pakoras and placing them in the basket, leaving space between each one so they don't touch.
6. **Spray** the tops of the pakoras generously with oil in the air fryer and cook for 4 minutes. Remove the air fryer basket, generously spray with oil, and fry for an additional 4 minutes.
7. **Remove** the basket and sprinkle the pakoras with oil again. Gently turn each one over. Spray the tops with oil and fry for 4 minutes. Remove the basket, spray generously with with oil one last time, and fry for a final 4 minutes, or until very browned and crisp. Serve immediately, plain or with some Cilantro Chutney.

Per Serving: Calories: 79; Total fat: 1g; Saturated fat: 0g; Cholesterol: 0mg; Sodium: 191mg; Carbohydrates: 13g; Fiber: 4g; Protein: 4g

Baked Potato

FAMILY-FRIENDLY / GLUTEN-FREE

SERVING	PREP TIME	COOK TIME	BAKE
2	5 mins	40 mins	400°F

INGREDIENTS

- **2 medium russet potatoes scrubbed clean**
- **¼ teaspoon sea salt**
- **½ teaspoon garlic powder (optional)**
- **¼ teaspoon black pepper (optional)**

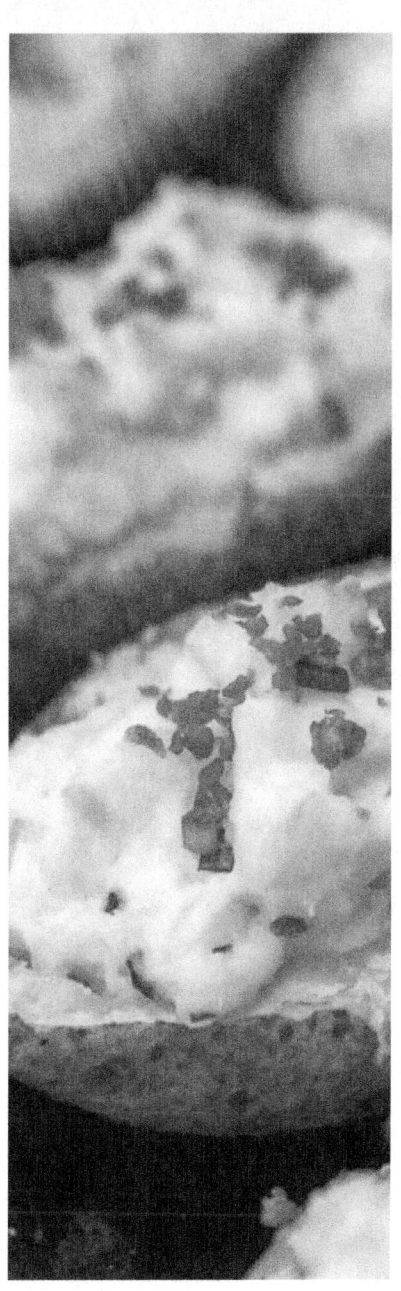

INSTRUCTIONS

1. **Rinse** and scrub your potatoes clean, poke a few holes with a fork or knife all around and then sprinkle them evenly with the seasoning on all sides. Place inside your fryer basket.
2. **Air** fry at 400 degrees F for 35-45 minutes, flipping them over around the 20 minute mark. (Use tongs to flip them.)
3. **Serve** warm with any of your favourite toppings.

Tips:
- Poke a few holes in your potatoes using a fork or knife all around before popping them into your fryer basket. Although it doesn't happen every time, the potatoes CAN explode from the steam build up.
- Season as desired. We like salt, pepper and garlic powder, but feel free to sub or omit any seasonings to your taste.
- Cook time will vary according to the size of your russet potatoes, and the model of air fryer you're using. When a fork pierces easily through your potato, it's ready.

Per Serving: Calories: 168cal; Carbohydrates: 38g; Protein: 5g; Saturated Fat: 1g; Sodium: 298mg; Potassium: 888mg; Fiber: 3g; Sugar: 1g; Calcium: 28mg; Iron: 2mg

Air Fried Pita Chips

FAST / FAMILY-FRIENDLY

SERVING	PREP TIME	COOK TIME	FRY
2	5 mins	3 mins	350°F

INGREDIENTS

- **2 whole wheat pita bread or your choice**
- **1 tablespoon aquafaba or oil of choice if preferred**
- **½ teaspoon garlic powder**
- **½ teaspoon dried parsley**
- **¼ teaspoon sea salt**

INSTRUCTIONS

1. **Cut** your pitas into 8 triangular wedges. Using a pizza cutter is a quick way to do this. Then combine the remaining ingredients in a small bowl.
2. **Brush** the spice mixture on the tops of your pita wedges. Then arrange them in your air frying basket. (It's okay if they overlap a bit.)
3. **Air** fry at 350°F/176°C for 3-4 minutes for softer chips OR 5-7 minutes for crispier chips. Check on them often and remove them when the desired doneness is reached.

Tips:
- Different air frying models cook at different speeds.
- Check on your chips often, starting at the 3-minute mark. For softer chips, air fry for approx. 3-4 minutes. For crispy chips, air fry for approx. 5-7 minutes.
- No problem for the pita triangles to overlap a bit in your fryer basket. However, don't completely overlap them. Work in batches, if needed.

Per Serving: Calories: 149cal; Carbohydrates: 32g; Protein: 6g; Sodium: 745mg; Potassium: 105mg; Fiber: 3g; Sugar: 2g; Calcium: 9mg; Iron: 2mg

Two Ways Carrots

FAST / FAMILY-FRIENDLY / GLUTEN-FREE

SERVING: 4
PREP TIME: 10 mins
COOK TIME: 15 mins
FRY: 400°F

INGREDIENTS

- **1 lb carrots peeled and chopped into 1 inch pieces**
- **3 tablespoon maple syrup**
- **1 teaspoon cinnamon**
- **¼ teaspoon sea salt**
- **1 tablespoon melted vegan butter or margarine optional**
- **2 tablespoon avocado oil or sub for veggie broth to make it oil free**
- **½ teaspoon garlic powder**
- **½ teaspoon sea salt**
- **½ teaspoon dried parsley**
- **¼ teaspoon ground black pepper**
- **⅛ teaspoon cayenne pepper**

INSTRUCTIONS

1. **Peel** and chop your carrots into approx. one inch pieces and place them in a mixing bowl.
2. **Depending** on which version you're making (sweet or spicy), add each of the ingredients to the bowl and mix well to evenly coat the carrots.
3. **For** the sweet version: Place the coated carrots in an oven safe dish that fits inside your air fryer basket. (So you don't lose all the syrup, and the carrots come more caramelized this way.)
4. **For** the spicy version: Transfer the coated carrots directly into the basket.
5. **Cook** at 400 degrees F for 15-18 minutes, or until tender.

Tips:
- Cut your carrots in uniform sized pieces for even cooking. If you have some larger pieces, they won't be as tender.
- Cooking time will vary depending on the model you're using, and the size you cut all your carrots, so check on the while they're cooking to get them just right.
- Use dried herbs over fresh as they tend to hold up better in this recipe.

Per Serving: Calories: 109cal; Carbohydrates: 21g; Protein: 1g; Saturated Fat: 1g; Sodium: 248mg; Potassium: 397mg; Fiber: 4g; Sugar: 14g; Calcium: 60mg; Iron: 1mg

Air Fried Green Tomatoes

FAST / GLUTEN-FREE

SERVING	PREP TIME	COOK TIME	FRY
4	8 mins	15 mins	392°F

INGREDIENTS

- ¾ cup cornmeal
- 2 tablespoons chickpea or brown rice flour
- 1 teaspoon seasoned salt
- 1 teaspoon onion granules
- ¼ teaspoon freshly ground black pepper
- ½ cup nondairy milk, plain and unsweetened
- Cooking oil spray (coconut, sunflower, or safflower)
- 2 large green (unripe) tomatoes, cut into ½-inch rounds

INSTRUCTIONS

1. **In** a medium bowl, combine the cornmeal, flour, seasoned salt, onion, and pepper, stirring well to incorporate. Set aside. Put the milk in another medium bowl and leave aside.
2. **Next**, start breading the tomatoes. Dip each tomato slice in milk, then lightly coat with cornmeal mixture, breading both sides.
3. **Place** the tomato back in the milk, followed by the breading. Apply a thorough coating to both sides.
4. **Place** the coated slices in the air fryer basket and spray with oil. Repeat with additional tomato slices, adding only enough to form a single layer. Spray the tops generously with oil until no dry breading remains. Fry for 6 minutes, then remove the air fryer basket.
5. **Spray** the tops again with oil, and then carefully turn each tomato slice over, being careful not to overlap too much. Spray generously with oil again until there are no dry patches. Fry for another three minutes. Remove the basket, spray with oil one last time (no need to flip them this time), and fry for another 3 to 6 minutes,

or until crisp and golden-browned. Remove to a plate. Finish any remaining tomatoes in batches until you're out of tomato slices. Enjoy while hot.

Per Serving: Calories: 162; Total fat: 2g; Saturated fat: 0g; Cholesterol: 0mg; Sodium: 561mg; Carbohydrates: 32g; Fiber: 4g; Protein: 5g

Cheesy French Fries with Shallots

GLUTEN-FREE

SERVING	PREP TIME	COOK TIME	FRY
3	15 mins	19 mins	392°F

INGREDIENTS

- Cooking oil spray (sunflower, safflower, or refined coconut)
- 1 large potato (russet or Yukon Gold), cut into ¼-inch-thick slices
- 1 teaspoon neutral-flavored oil (sunflower, safflower, or refined coconut)
- ¼ teaspoon sea salt
- ⅛ teaspoon freshly ground black pepper
- 1 large shallot, thinly sliced
- ½ cup plus 2 tablespoons prepared Cheesy Sauce
- 2 tablespoons minced chives or scallions (optional)

INSTRUCTIONS

1. **Spray** the air fryer basket with oil. Set aside.
2. **In** a medium bowl, combine the potato pieces, oil, salt, and pepper. Place in air fryer basket and cook for 6 minutes. Remove the air fryer basket, mix or shake (to ensure that the slices cook uniformly), and fry for an additional 4 minutes.
3. **Remove**. Add the shallots, stir (or shake), and cook for another 5 minutes.
4. **Make** the Cheesy Sauce according to the instructions. Set aside or keep warm on a low-temperature burner.
5. **Remove** the air fryer basket, mix or shake, and cook for a further 4 minutes, or until the fries and shallots are crisp and golden. Serve topped with Cheesy Sauce and a sprinkle of chives or scallions.

Tips:
- Optional toppings include vegan bacon (tempeh or coconut) or jalapeño slices.

Per Serving: Calories: 73; Total fat: 1g; Saturated fat: 0g; Cholesterol: 0mg; Sodium: 93mg; Carbohydrates: 15g; Fiber: 2g; Protein: 2g

Air Fried Cabbage

FAST / FAMILY-FRIENDLY / GLUTEN-FREE

SERVING	PREP TIME	COOK TIME	FRY
2	5 mins	10 mins	360°F

INGREDIENTS

- **Half of a medium head of green cabbage - about 12 ounces**
- **1 large lemon**
- **1 teaspoon Cajun seasoning - or another spice blend, such as harissa, za'atar, or curry powder**
- **salt and pepper, to taste**

INSTRUCTIONS

1. **Remove** the grate from the bottom of your air fryer basket, and add ½ cup water. Put the grate back in place, and preheat the air fryer to 360°F (182°C).
2. **If** you're starting with a whole head of cabbage, discard loose or wilted leaves from the exterior, and trim off the very bottom of the core. You now have a flat base to rest against the cutting board for stability. For cabbage steaks, slice from the top down into 1-inch thick slices (it's easiest to start near the center and work your way out). For wedges, slice the cabbage in half through the core. Then slice one of the halves into 4 or 5 equal-size wedges so that each piece has some core holding it together. Save the other half of the cabbage for another dish, or prepare two batches in the air fryer.
3. **Coat** both sides of the wedges/steaks with lemon juice, then sprinkle with your seasoning of choice and a few generous pinches of salt and pepper.
4. **Arrange** in a single layer the air fryer. Cook for 8 to 10 minutes or until the cabbage is crisp-tender and charred around the edges. You can flip the cabbage at the halfway point if you like, but it isn't necessary.
5. **Serve** hot with an extra squeeze of fresh lemon. Enjoy the cabbage leaves, but discard the core if it's too tough.

Per Serving: Calories: 40kcal; Carbohydrates: 7g; Protein: 2g; Fat: 0g; Cholesterol: 0mg

Air Fry Away to Delicious

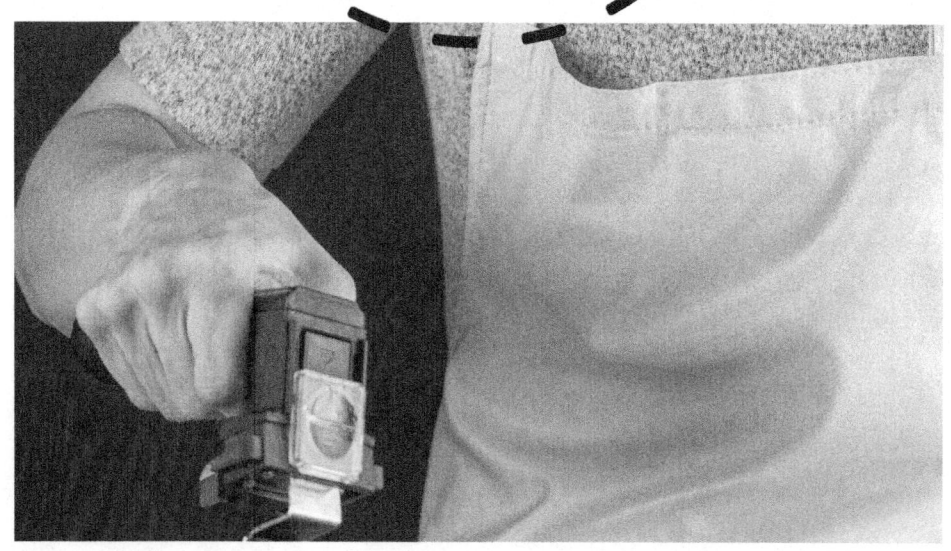

4
Main Dishes

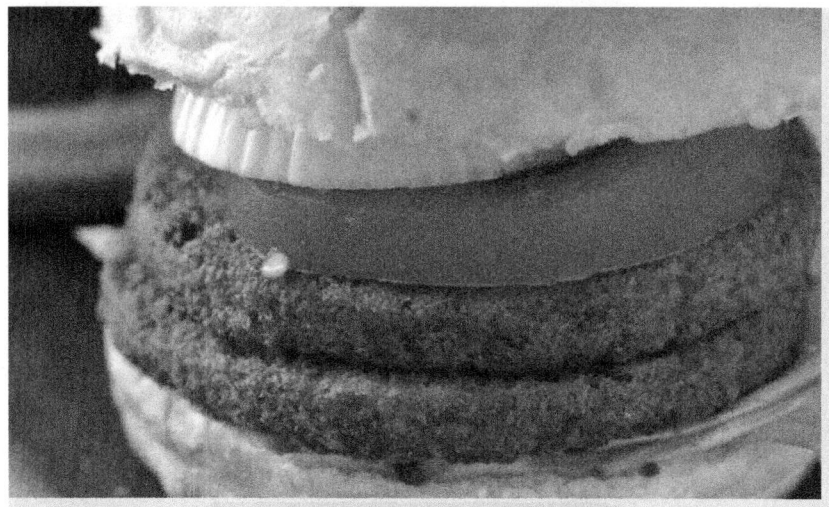

FAST / FAMILY-FRIENDLY

SERVING	PREP TIME	COOK TIME	FRY
4	10 mins	12 mins	350°F

INGREDIENTS

- **1 cup TVP (textured vegetable protein)**
- **⅔ cup hot water**
- **¾ cup cooked black beans or kidney beans, rinsed, drained and patted dry**
- **2 tablespoons nutritional yeast**
- **1 ½ tablespoons soy sauce - or tamari for Gluten-free**
- **1 tablespoon apple cider vinegar**
- **1 tablespoon oil, optional - or smooth raw almond butter**
- **2 teaspoons sriracha hot sauce - or ketchup or BBQ sauce**
- **1 teaspoon garlic powder**
- **1 teaspoon smoked paprika**
- **1 teaspoon dried parsley, optional**
- **½ teaspoon dried oregano**
- **½ teaspoon onion powder**
- **¼ cup vital wheat gluten**

INSTRUCTIONS

1. **Preheat** air fryer to 350 degrees F or oven to 370 degrees F.
2. **Combine** TVP and hot water in a bowl and stir well.
3. **In** a mixing bowl, mash the beans with a fork. Add the hydrated TVP and all remaining ingredients except the flour/vital wheat gluten. Stir to combine.
4. **Add** the vital wheat gluten/flour to the bowl and stir. Now use your hands to make sure everything is well incorporated. Lightly knead and mix for 30 seconds or so, to develop the gluten.
5. **Form** the mixture into a rectangle and divide evenly into 4 pieces. Shape each piece into a patty about ⅝-inch thick. Note: flatter/thinner burgers will be firmer and more dry; slightly thicker patties will be softer and more moist inside. We like them both ways!
6. **Air** fry for 11 to 13 minutes, flipping at the halfway point. The burgers are done when firm, crisp around the edges, and piping hot in the center.
7. **Let** cool for a few minutes then serve on a bun or in a grain bowl or salad.

Per Serving: Calories: 188kcal; Carbohydrates: 17g; Protein: 23g; Fat: 4g; Fiber: 6g

Vegan Cauliflower Buffalo Wings

FAMILY-FRIENDLY / GLUTEN-FREE

SERVING	PREP TIME	COOK TIME	FRY
4	25 mins	30 mins	390°F

INGREDIENTS

- 1 small cauliflower cut into small bite sized florets
- ½ cup brown rice flour or flour of choice if not avoiding gluten
- 1 teaspoon garlic powder
- 1 teaspoon onion powder
- 1.5 teaspoon paprika
- ½ teaspoon cumin
- ½ teaspoon sea salt
- ¼ teaspoon black pepper
- ¼ teaspoon cayenne pepper
- ¾ cup unsweetened cashew milk or milk of choice
- ½ cup water
- ¼ cup white vinegar
- 1 teaspoon paprika
- 1 teaspoon garlic powder
- ¼ teaspoon cayenne pepper
- ½ teaspoon sea salt
- 3 tablespoon tomato paste

INSTRUCTIONS

1. **Place** your cut up cauliflower in a large bowl. Then in a separate bowl, combine your flour and all the seasonings and mix to combine. Then add the milk and mix well to make your batter. Now pour the batter into your bowl with the cauliflower and mix well to evenly coat each piece.
2. **Place** your coated cauliflower into your crisp basket. Then set it to 390 degrees F and air fry for 20 minutes, shaking your basket every 5 minutes or so.
3. **Meanwhile**, prepare your buffalo wing sauce by adding all its ingredients to a small sauce pan. Whisk to combine and simmer over medium heat 3-5 minutes, allowing the flavours to combine.
4. **Then** use a silicone brush to evenly coat your florets in the buffalo sauce. Continue air frying for another 10-15 minutes, shaking or flipping your florets at the halfway point. Cook time will vary according to the air fryer model you're using and floret size.
5. **Serve** with ranch and dunk away.

Per Serving: Calories: 118cal; Carbohydrates: 23g; Protein: 4g; Sodium: 732mg; Potassium: 440mg; Fiber: 4g; Sugar: 3g; Calcium: 32mg; Iron: 2mg

Spaghetti Squash

FAST / FAMILY-FRIENDLY

SERVING	PREP TIME	COOK TIME	FRY
2	5 mins	20 mins	360°F

INGREDIENTS

- **2 lb spaghetti squash (1 small squash, but weigh for most accurate results)**
- **2 teaspoon avocado oil or your choice**
- **½ teaspoon sea salt**
- **¼ teaspoon black pepper**
- **¼ teaspoon garlic powder**
- **¼ teaspoon smoked paprika**
- **<u>Vegan Parmesan cheese</u> (optional)**
- **Fresh parsley (optional)**

INSTRUCTIONS

1. **Cut** a thin slice off the ends of your squash and then cut in half, lengthwise, as evenly as possible in two halves. Place the two halves in your air fryer basket, cut side up. Then drizzle with the oil (if using) and evenly sprinkle with the seasoning.
2. **Cook** at 360 degrees F for 20 minutes, or until a fork can easily pierce the flesh. (This may vary according to the size of your squash.)
3. **Once** cooked, transfer to a dish and fluff up the inside with a fork. Then add the parmesan cheese and fresh parsley, if using, and enjoy.

Per Serving: Calories: 142cal; Carbohydrates: 23g; Protein: 2g; Saturated Fat: 1g; Sodium: 637mg; Fiber: 5g; Sugar: 9g; Calcium: 74mg; Iron: 1mg

Air Fried Mushrooms

FAST / FAMILY-FRIENDLY

SERVING	PREP TIME	COOK TIME	ROAST
4	5 mins	8 mins	390°F

INGREDIENTS

- **16 oz cremini mushrooms clean & dry, halved**
- **2 tablespoon low sodium tamari or soy sauce if not avoiding gluten**
- **2 tablespoon lemon juice approx half a medium lemon**
- **1 teaspoon garlic powder**
- **0.25 teaspoon black pepper optional**

INSTRUCTIONS

1. **Cut** your clean and dry mushrooms in half (or quarters if they're large) and lay them in a basin. Add the other ingredients to the bowl and mix thoroughly.
2. **Place** them in the air fryer basket and cook at 390 degrees F for 8-10 minutes. Shake the basket or stir the mushrooms every couple minutes.

Tips:
- Shake or stir your mushrooms every few minutes while cooking to prevent sticking and ensure they brown evenly.
- Don't chop the mushrooms too small. Simply split them in half because they will decrease significantly after cooking. If your mushrooms are particularly huge, you can chop them into quarters.
- Try not to put too many mushrooms in your cart. Because they emit a lot of water while cooking, you don't want them to steam. So, arrange in a single layer.

Per Serving: Calories: 33cal; Carbohydrates: 7g; Protein: 3g; Fat: 1g; Sodium: 274mg; Potassium: 508mg; Fiber: 1g; Calcium: 20mg; Iron: 1mg

Panang Curry Bowl

GLUTEN-FREE

SERVING: 4
PREP TIME: 15 mins
COOK TIME: 20 mins *(plus time for rice or noodles)*
FRY: 392°F

INGREDIENTS

- 4 cups cooked rice or rice noodles, any variety
- Sesame Crunch Tofu or Crisp Tofu
- 1 (14-ounce) can full-fat coconut milk
- ¼ cup plus 2 tablespoons coconut sugar
- ¼ cup red curry paste
- ¼ cup natural peanut butter
- 2 tablespoons coconut oil
- 4 large garlic cloves, peeled
- 1 teaspoon sea salt
- 1 teaspoon grated lime zest
- 4 cups chopped vegetables, your choice
- Sesame seeds, black or regular, for topping (optional)

INSTRUCTIONS

1. **If** you haven't cooked the noodles or rice yet, you should do it right away. Just be mindful of how long they need to simmer in relation to the remaining ingredients.
2. **Next**, get the tofu ready and start frying it in the air fryer as directed by the recipe.
3. **Prepare** the sauce while the tofu cooks: The coconut milk, coconut sugar, red curry paste, peanut butter, coconut oil, garlic, salt, and lime zest should all be combined in a blender jar and blended until extremely smooth. Put aside. (If you have leftovers, which you may, they will keep for at least a week in the refrigerator when stored in an airtight container.)
4. **Prepare** your vegetables (air fry broccoli and cauliflower for 5 to 8 minutes at 392°F) and set them aside.
5. **When** the tofu is almost done, you might want to reheat the panang sauce on the stovetop over low heat until it's hot.
6. **To** serve, fill your bowls with cooked rice or noodles and top with the vegetables. Add a liberal amount of sauce and place tofu chunks on top. If used, sprinkle with sesame seeds.

Per Serving: Calories: 894; Total fat: 57g; Saturated fat: 31g; Cholesterol: 0mg; Sodium: 1378mg; Carbohydrates: 86g; Fiber: 9g; Protein: 16g

Red Curry Noodles with Sesame Crunch Tofu

GLUTEN-FREE

SERVING	PREP TIME	COOK TIME	FRY
4	20 mins	20 mins	392°F

INGREDIENTS

- **Sesame Crunch Tofu**
- **1 (8-ounce) package Thai rice noodles (preferably brown rice noodles)**
- **2 tablespoons Thai red curry paste**
- **1 (14-ounce) can full-fat coconut milk, divided**
- **4 large garlic cloves, pressed or finely minced**
- **2 tablespoons grated fresh ginger**
- **¼ cup fresh lime juice**
- **1 teaspoon sea salt**
- **⅓ cup chopped cilantro**
- **⅓ cup chopped fresh basil**
- **⅓ cup minced scallions**
- **⅓ cup finely chopped red cabbage**

INSTRUCTIONS

1. **Get** the Sesame Crunch Tofu ready.
2. **While** it is in the air fryer, prepare the rest of the dish. Begin by cooking the noodles according to the directions on the package.
3. **While** the noodles cook, prepare the sauce: In a large bowl, combine curry paste and 1/4 cup coconut milk. Using a wire whisk or a fork, combine the ingredients until smooth. Add the remaining coconut milk and stir until emulsified. Combine the garlic, ginger, lime juice, and salt. Stir or whisk thoroughly.
4. **Add** the cilantro, basil, scallions, and cabbage to the bowl and mix.
5. **Once** the noodles are al dente, drain them thoroughly and place them in the bowl. Stir slowly to fully incorporate the sauce. Serve the noodle-vegetable mixture hot, topped with Sesame Crunch Tofu.

Per Serving: Calories: 607; Total fat: 40g; Saturated fat: 27g; Cholesterol: 0mg; Sodium: 1256mg; Carbohydrates: 59g; Fiber: 6g; Protein: 10g

Eggplant Parmigiana

FAMILY-FRIENDLY / GLUTEN-FREE

SERVING	PREP TIME	COOK TIME	FRY
4	15 mins	40 mins	392°F

INGREDIENTS

- **1 medium eggplant (about 1 pound), sliced into ½-inch-thick rounds**
- **2 tablespoons tamari or shoyu**
- **3 tablespoons nondairy milk, plain and unsweetened**
- **1 cup chickpea flour**
- **1 tablespoon dried basil**
- **1 tablespoon dried oregano**
- **2 teaspoons garlic granules**
- **2 teaspoons onion granules**
- **½ teaspoon sea salt**
- **½ teaspoon ground black pepper**
- **Cooking oil spray (sunflower, safflower, or refined coconut)**
- **Vegan marinara sauce (your choice)**
- **Shredded vegan cheese**

INSTRUCTIONS

1. **In** a large bowl, combine the eggplant pieces, tamari, and milk. Turn the pieces over to ensure that they are uniformly coated with the liquids. Set aside.
2. **Make** the coating. In a medium bowl, add the flour, basil, oregano, garlic, onion, salt, and pepper. Stir thoroughly. Set aside.
3. **Spray** the air fryer basket with oil and set it aside.
4. **Stir** the eggplant slices again and transfer to a platter (stacking is acceptable). Do not discard the liquid in the dish.
5. **To** bread the eggplant, toss one eggplant round in the flour mixture. Then, take another dip in the liquid. Double up on the coating by dipping the eggplant again in the flour mixture, ensuring that all sides are well coated. Place in an air fryer basket.
6. **Repeat** with enough eggplant rounds to form (basically) a single layer in the air fryer basket. (You'll need to cook it in batches to avoid overlap and ensure it cooks precisely.)
7. **Spray** the eggplant tops with enough oil to remove any dry patches in the coating. Fry for eight minutes. Remove the air fryer basket and respray the tops. Turn each piece over, being careful not to overlap the rounds too much. Spray the tops with oil again, making sure there are no dry patches. Fry for an additional 8 minutes, or until beautifully browned and crispy.
8. **Place** half of the eggplant in a 6-inch round, 2-inch deep baking pan, then top with marinara and vegan cheese. Fry for 3 minutes, or until the sauce is heated and the cheese has melted (avoid overcooking or the eggplant edges will burn). Serve immediately, simple or with spaghetti.

Per Serving: Calories: 217; Total fat: 9g; Saturated fat: 1g; Cholesterol: 0mg; Sodium: 903mg; Carbohydrates: 38g; Fiber: 10g; Protein: 9g

BBQ Jackfruit Nachos

FAMILY-FRIENDLY / GLUTEN-FREE

SERVING	PREP TIME	COOK TIME	FRY
3	30 mins	20 mins	347°F

INGREDIENTS

- 1 (20-ounce) can jackfruit, drained
- ⅓ cup prepared vegan BBQ sauce
- ¼ cup water
- 2 tablespoons tamari or shoyu
- 1 tablespoon fresh lemon juice
- 4 large garlic cloves
- 1 teaspoon onion granules
- ⅛ teaspoon cayenne powder
- ⅛ teaspoon liquid smoke
- Double batch Garlic Lime Tortilla Chips
- 2½ cups prepared Cheesy Sauce
- 3 medium-size tomatoes, chopped
- ¾ cup guacamole of your choice
- ¾ cup chopped cilantro
- ½ cup minced red onion
- 1 jalapeño, seeds removed and thinly sliced (optional)

INSTRUCTIONS

1. **In** a large skillet over high heat, combine the jackfruit, BBQ sauce, water, tamari, lemon juice, garlic, onion granules, cayenne pepper, and liquid smoke. Stir thoroughly and break up the jackfruit with a spatula.
2. **Once** the mixture has boiled, turn the heat down to low. Continue to cook, stirring frequently (and breaking up the jackfruit as you go), for about 20 minutes, or until the liquid has been absorbed. Remove from heat and set aside.
3. **Assemble** the nachos: Place chips on three plates and top with jackfruit mixture, warmed Cheesy Sauce, tomatoes, guacamole, cilantro, onion, and jalapeño (if using). Soggy chips are terrible, so eat them right away.

Per Serving: Calories: 661; Total fat: 15g; Saturated fat: 1g; Cholesterol: 0mg; Sodium: 1842mg; Carbohydrates: 124g; Fiber: 19g; Protein: 22g

GLUTEN-FREE

SERVING	PREP TIME	COOK TIME	FRY
3	25 mins	20 mins	392°F

Ginger Tahini Noodles with Sesame Crunch Tofu

INGREDIENTS

- **Sesame Crunch Tofu**
- **1 (5.29-ounce) package bean thread noodles (3 "nests")**
- **3 tablespoons mellow white miso**
- **3 tablespoons tahini (ground sesame paste)**
- **3 tablespoons fresh lime juice**
- **3 tablespoons grated fresh ginger**
- **5 large garlic cloves**
- **1½ cups finely chopped cabbage (red or green, your choice)**
- **1½ cups diced cucumber**
- **½ cup chopped cilantro**
- **⅓ cup finely chopped scallions**

INSTRUCTIONS

1. **Prepare** the Sesame Crunch Tofu.
2. **While** the tofu cooks, you may prepare the rest of the dish. Begin by cooking the noodles as directed on the packet. (To make bean threads, bring water to a boil, add the nests, cover, and let sit for 5 minutes—or until the noodles are soft.
3. **In** a large bowl, combine the miso, tahini, and lime juice. Using a wire whisk or fork, stir until well combined. Add the ginger and garlic, and sauté again.
4. **Place** the cabbage, cucumber, cilantro, and scallions in the bowl. Add the noodles to the bowl and mix thoroughly. Serve topped with tofu.

Per Serving: Calories: 549; Total fat: 26g; Saturated fat: 1g; Cholesterol: 0mg; Sodium: 1805mg; Carbohydrates: 70g; Fiber: 6g; Protein: 8g

Cauliflower Steak

GLUTEN-FREE

SERVING: 4
PREP TIME: 10 mins
COOK TIME: 15 mins
FRY: 375°F

INGREDIENTS

- 2 large cauliflower
- 4 tablespoons vegetable broth
- 2 tablespoon lime juice approx. half a lime
- 2 teaspoon smoked paprika
- 2 teaspoon garlic powder
- 1 teaspoon sea salt
- 0.5 teaspoon black pepper

INSTRUCTIONS

1. **Wash** the cauliflower head and remove the green leaves, but do not cut the stem.
2. **Then**, place the cauliflower stem side down on a chopping board and trim both ends to make them flat, reserving any loose pieces that come off.
3. **Now**, cut the remaining portion into 2 or 3 steaks (depending on the size of your cauliflower head) using thick slices (about 1.25 inch thick).
4. **In** a small bowl, add all of the marinade ingredients and whisk thoroughly. Then brush one side of each steak, place it sauce side down in the air fryer basket, and brush the other side.
5. **Air** fry for 10 minutes at 375°F/190°C, then carefully flip the steaks and cook for another 5-8 minutes, or until the cauliflower is tender and golden brown.

Tips:
- For consistent cooking, use a sharp knife to cut cauliflower steaks that are around the same size.
- To save time, you can buy pre-cut cauliflower steaks at the grocery.

Per Serving: Calories: 118cal; Carbohydrates: 24g; Protein: 9g; Fat: 1g; Sodium: 826mg; Potassium: 1320mg; Fiber: 9g; Calcium: 99mg; Iron: 3mg

5
Desserts

Pineapple Upside-Down Cake

FAMILY-FRIENDLY

SERVING	PREP TIME	COOK TIME	BAKE
6	10 mins	30 mins	320°F

INGREDIENTS

- 1 cup whole-wheat pastry flour
- 1½ tablespoons ground flaxseed
- ½ teaspoon plus ⅛ teaspoon baking soda
- ¼ teaspoon sea salt
- ½ cup pineapple juice, fresh or canned
- 2 tablespoons melted coconut oil (plus more for greasing your pan)
- ¼ cup plus 2 tablespoons agave nectar
- ½ tablespoon fresh lemon juice
- 1 teaspoon vanilla
- 1 to 2 tablespoons coconut sugar (for coating the pan)
- 3 pineapple rings (fresh or canned)
- Vanilla or coconut vegan ice cream (optional)
- Vegan whipped topping (optional)

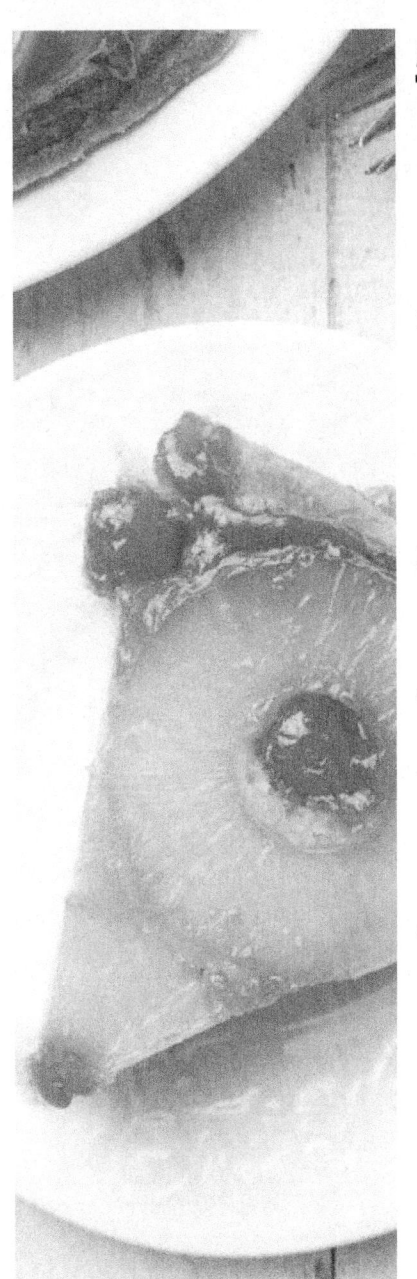

INSTRUCTIONS

1. **In** a larger basin, combine the flour, flaxmeal, baking soda, and salt. Whisk thoroughly. Combine the pineapple juice, oil, agave, lemon juice, and vanilla. Stir only until well blended.
2. **Preheat** the air fryer for two minutes. Coat the bottom and sides of a 6-inch round, 2-inch deep baking pan with coconut oil. Sprinkle coconut sugar evenly over the bottom of the pan (enough to gently coat it).
3. **Place** the pineapple rings in a single layer on top of the sugar (some may need to be broken up). Pour the batter on top of the pineapple rings.
4. **Carefully** place the pan in your preheated air fryer. Bake for 25–30 minutes, or until a knife inserted into the center comes out clean. Note: Your cake may appear done before the middle is fully cooked, so use the knife test.
5. **Carefully** remove the pan and let it cool on a plate or wire rack for 3 to 5 minutes. Run a knife down the pan's edges. Place a dish on top (so that it touches the exposed cake). Gently flip the cake upside down on the plate. Next, gently remove the baking pan from the cake, leaving the pineapple rings on top. Cut and serve simple, with vegan ice cream, or with whipped topping.

Per Serving: Calories: 191; Total fat: 5g; Saturated fat: 4g; Cholesterol: 0mg; Sodium: 183mg; Carbohydrates: 35g; Fiber: 4g; Protein: 2g

Air Fryer Strawberries

FAMILY-FRIENDLY / GLUTEN-FREE

SERVING	PREP TIME	COOK TIME	FRY
4	5 mins	1 hour	190°F

INGREDIENTS

- **600 grams fresh strawberries**

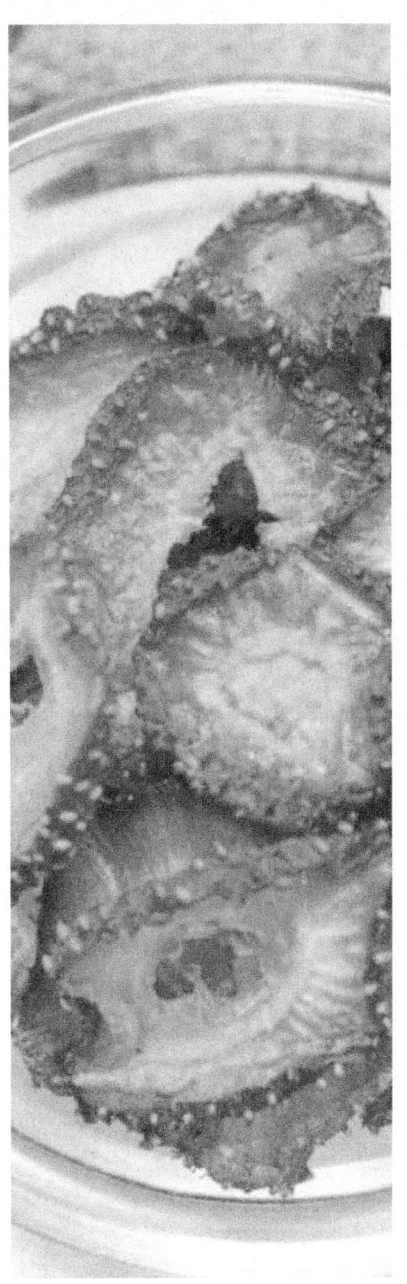

INSTRUCTIONS

1. **Wash** the strawberries and pat them dry to remove any excess moisture. Then, hull/remove the stems with a strawberry huller or a sharp knife.
2. **Slice** the berries uniformly, about ⅛ inch thick. Then, put them in a single layer in the air fryer basket, avoiding overlapping.
3. **Cook** at 190°F/88°C for 60-90 minutes to air fry or dehydrate (depending on model). (Time will vary depending on the thickness of your slices and the air frying model you use.)
4. **After** 45 minutes, check on your strawberries and flip them. Then check on them every 15 minutes until they are completely dry to the touch.

Tips:
- Thick slices will take longer to dry than narrow slices. To ensure even cooking periods, try to cut the berries with a regular thickness.
- Once done, remove the thinner parts and continue cooking the thicker pieces until each slice is dehydrated.

Per Serving: Calories: 248; Total fat: 8g; Saturated fat: 1g; Cholesterol: 0mg; Sodium: 61mg; Carbohydrates: 42g; Fiber: 6g; Protein: 3g

Vegan Lemon Bars

GLUTEN-FREE

SERVING: 6
PREP TIME: 15 mins
COOK TIME: 25 mins
BAKE: 347°F

INGREDIENTS

- ¾ cup whole-wheat pastry flour
- 2 tablespoons powdered sugar
- ¼ cup refined coconut oil, melted
- ½ cup organic sugar
- 1 packed tablespoon lemon zest
- ¼ cup fresh lemon juice
- ⅛ teaspoon sea salt
- ¼ cup unsweetened, plain applesauce
- 1¾ teaspoons arrowroot (or cornstarch)
- ¾ teaspoon baking powder
- Cooking oil spray (sunflower, safflower, or refined coconut)

INSTRUCTIONS

1. **To** prepare the crust: Combine the flour, powdered sugar, and oil in a small basin, stirring just until incorporated. Place in the refrigerator.
2. **To** prepare the filling: In a larger bowl, combine the sugar, lemon zest and juice, salt, applesauce, arrowroot, and baking powder. Stir thoroughly.
3. **Coat** a 6-inch round, 2-inch deep baking pan gently with oil. Take the crust mixture out of the fridge and carefully press it into the bottom of the pan to make a crust. Place in the air fryer and cook for 5 minutes, or until slightly firm to the touch.
4. **Remove** and spread the lemon filling over the crust. Bake for approximately 18 to 20 minutes, or until the top is well browned. Allow to cool in the refrigerator for at least an hour. When stiff and cooled, cut into pieces to serve. You may need to use a fork to remove each piece because the pan is too small for typical spatulas.

Per Serving: Calories: 202; Total fat: 9g; Saturated fat: 8g; Cholesterol: 0mg; Sodium: 3mg; Carbohydrates: 30g; Fiber: 2g; Protein: 1g

Chocolate Chip Cookies

FAST / FAMILY-FRIENDLY / GLUTEN-FREE

MAKE
6
cookies

PREP TIME
10
mins

COOK TIME
7
mins

BAKE
347°F

INGREDIENTS

- **1 tablespoon refined coconut oil, melted**
- **1 tablespoon maple syrup**
- **1 tablespoon nondairy milk**
- **½ teaspoon vanilla**
- **¼ cup plus 2 tablespoons whole-wheat pastry flour or all-purpose gluten-free flour**
- **2 tablespoons coconut sugar**
- **¼ teaspoon sea salt**
- **¼ teaspoon baking powder**
- **2 tablespoons vegan chocolate chips**
- **Cooking oil spray (sunflower, safflower, or refined coconut)**

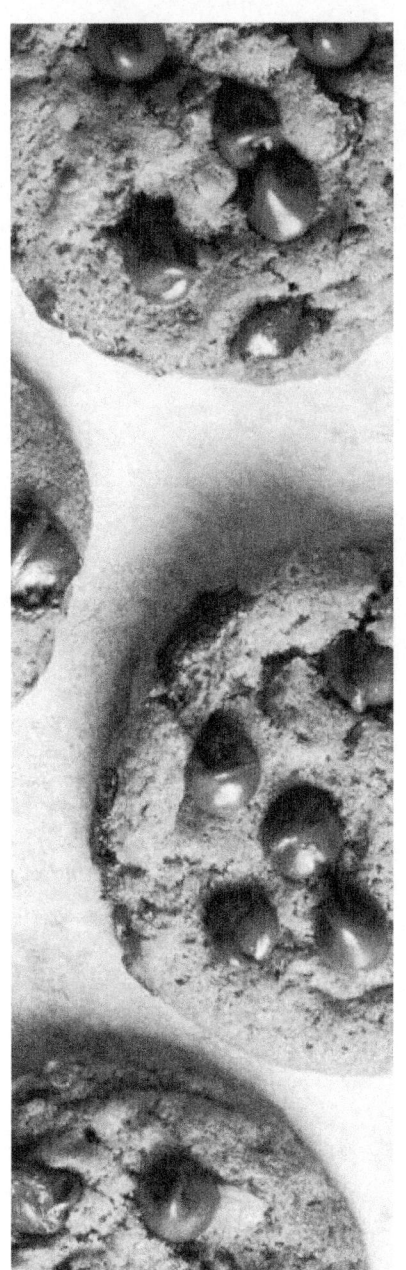

INSTRUCTIONS

1. **In** a medium bowl, combine the oil, maple syrup, milk, and vanilla. Combine flour, coconut sugar, salt, and baking powder. Stir only until well blended. Stir in the chocolate chips.
2. **Preheat** the air fryer basket (which contains a 6-inch round, 2-inch deep baking pan) for 2 minutes. Then, spray the pan lightly with oil. Drop tablespoonfuls of batter onto the pan, leaving some space between them in case they spread. Bake for 7 minutes, or until light brown. Take care not to overcook.
3. **Gently** transfer to a cooling rack or dish. Repeat as desired, either baking all of the cookies at once or storing the batter in the fridge for later use. If possible, enjoy it warm!

Per Serving: Calories: 71; Total fat: 3g; Saturated fat: 2g; Cholesterol: 0mg; Sodium: 81mg; Carbohydrates: 11g; Fiber: 1g; Protein: 1g

Oatmeal Raisin Cookies

FAST / FAMILY-FRIENDLY / GLUTEN-FREE

MAKE	PREP TIME	COOK TIME	BAKE
18 cookies	10 mins	7 mins	347°F

INGREDIENTS

- ¼ cup plus ½ tablespoon vegan margarine
- 2½ tablespoons nondairy milk, plain and unsweetened
- ½ cup organic sugar
- ½ teaspoon vanilla extract
- ½ teaspoon plus ⅛ teaspoon ground cinnamon
- ½ cup plus 2 tablespoons flour (whole-wheat pastry, gluten-free all-purpose, or all-purpose)
- ¼ teaspoon sea salt
- ¾ cup rolled oats
- ¼ teaspoon baking soda
- ¼ teaspoon baking powder
- 2 tablespoons raisins
- Cooking oil spray (sunflower, safflower, or refined coconut)

INSTRUCTIONS

1. **Whip** the margarine in a medium bowl with an electric mixer until frothy.
2. **Mix** in the milk, sugar, and vanilla. Using beaters, stir or whip until thoroughly blended.
3. **In** a separate basin, whisk together the cinnamon, flour, salt, oats, baking soda, and baking powder. Add the dry mixture to the wet mixture and stir thoroughly with a wooden spoon. Stir in the raisins.
4. **Preheat** the air fryer basket (with a 6-inch round, 2-inch deep baking pan within) for 2 minutes. Then, spray the pan lightly with oil. Drop tablespoonfuls of batter into the pan, giving enough space between each one to allow for some spreading. Bake for approximately 7 minutes, or until gently browned.
5. **Transfer** to a cooling rack (or plate), taking care to keep the cookies intact. Making all of the cookies at once, or storing the batter in the fridge for later use (it will stay refrigerated in an airtight container for a week to 10 days).

Per Serving: Calories: 78; Total fat: 4g; Saturated fat: 1g; Cholesterol: 0mg; Sodium: 82mg; Carbohydrates: 11g; Fiber: 1g; Protein: 1g

Vegan Chocolate Cake

FAMILY-FRIENDLY / GLUTEN-FREE

SERVING	PREP TIME	COOK TIME	BAKE
6	10 mins	25 mins	347°F

INGREDIENTS

- ¾ cup flour (whole-wheat pastry, gluten-free all-purpose, or all-purpose)
- ½ cup organic sugar
- 2 tablespoons cocoa powder
- ½ teaspoon baking soda
- ⅛ teaspoon sea salt
- For the frosting
- 3 tablespoons vegan margarine
- 1¼ cups powdered sugar
- ½ cup nondairy milk
- 2½ tablespoons neutral flavored oil (sunflower, safflower, or melted refined coconut)
- ½ tablespoon apple cider vinegar
- ½ teaspoon vanilla
- Coconut oil (for greasing)
- 5 tablespoons cocoa powder
- 2 teaspoons vanilla
- ⅛ teaspoon sea salt

INSTRUCTIONS

1. **To** create the cake: Combine the flour, sugar, cocoa powder, baking soda, and salt in a medium basin and stir with a wire whisk. Once fully blended, add the milk, oil, vinegar, and vanilla. Stir just until thoroughly blended.
2. **Preheat** the air fryer for two minutes.
3. **Coat** a 6-inch round, 2-inch deep baking pan liberally with coconut oil. Place the batter in the oiled pan and bake for 25 minutes, or until a knife inserted in the center comes out clean.
4. **To** make frosting: Cream together the vegan margarine and powdered sugar in a medium bowl using an electric mixer. Add the cocoa powder, vanilla, and salt, and beat with the beaters until well incorporated and frothy. Refrigerate until ready for use.
5. **After** the cake has cooled fully, run a knife along the edges of the baking pan. Turn it upside down on a dish and ice the sides and top.
6. **Allow** the cake to cool for approximately 10 minutes, or until it is no longer hot. Once the frosting is no longer cold, coat the sides and top with a butter knife or small spatula. Cut into pieces and enjoy.

Per Serving: Calories: 341; Total fat: 13g; Saturated fat: 2g; Cholesterol: 0mg; Sodium: 280mg; Carbohydrates: 56g; Fiber: 4g; Protein: 3g

Air Fried Bananas

FAST / FAMILY-FRIENDLY / GLUTEN-FREE

SERVING	PREP TIME	COOK TIME	FRY
4	5 mins	8 mins	350°F

INGREDIENTS

- **4 small green bananas (or 1 large)**
- **2 tablespoon lemon juice approx. half a small lemon**
- **1 teaspoon sea salt**
- **0.5 teaspoon black pepper**

INSTRUCTIONS

1. **In** a small mixing bowl, combine the lemon juice, salt, and pepper; leave aside.
2. **Peel** and slice bananas into about ⅛ inch thick slices. A little thicker is good, but try to keep the slices uniform for even cooking. Then, lay the slices in the bowl with the marinade and gently stir to coat them evenly.
3. **Brush** a little oil into the air frying basket and arrange the bananas in a single layer. Then, air fried at 350 degrees Fahrenheit for 8-10 minutes, until golden and caramelized. To avoid burning, keep an eye on the food at the conclusion of the cooking process.

Tips:
- Slice your bananas as uniformly as possible to ensure even frying.
- If some of the slices are too thin, they may burn, so keep an eye on them at the end of the cooking time.

Per Serving: Calories: 92cal; Carbohydrates: 24g; Protein: 1g; Sodium: 583mg; Potassium: 373mg; Fiber: 3g; Sugar: 12g; Calcium: 7mg; Iron: 1mg

Baked Apples

FAST / FAMILY-FRIENDLY / GLUTEN-FREE

SERVING
4

PREP TIME
5
mins

COOK TIME
12
mins

BAKE
380°F

INGREDIENTS

- **4 large apples**
- **3 tablespoons maple syrup**
- **1 tablespoon vegan butter or margarine melted (optional)**
- **1 teaspoon cinnamon**
- **1 tablespoon tapioca starch or corn starch**

INSTRUCTIONS

1. **In** a medium bowl, mix together the syrup, melted butter (if using), cinnamon, and tapioca starch. Mix well.
2. **Wash** your apples, remove any stickers, and cut each into 8 wedges/segments, removing the seeds and core. Mix the sliced apple wedges into the bowl until evenly coated.
3. **Add** ¼ cup water to the bottom of your air fryer, underneath the basket. Then, arrange the coated apples in a uniform layer within the basket. Air fried the apples at 380 degrees Fahrenheit for 12-15 minutes, or until fork-tender. Stir every 5 minutes or such. Serve warm.

Tips:

- If you have picky eaters, remove the apple skin before slicing and coating with marinade for a smoother texture.
- Try to chop your apple wedges into equal-sized pieces for even cooking. If some portions are larger, they will be less soft.
- Keep leftovers in an airtight jar in the refrigerator for 1-2 days.

Per Serving: Calories: 164cal; Carbohydrates: 43g; Protein: 1g; Fat: 1g; Sodium: 4mg; Potassium: 275mg; Fiber: 6g; Sugar: 32g; Calcium: 35mg; Iron: 1mg

Air Fried Peaches

FAST / FAMILY-FRIENDLY / GLUTEN-FREE

SERVING	PREP TIME	COOK TIME	FRY
3	5 mins	8 mins	350°F

INGREDIENTS

- **1 pound fresh ripe but firm peaches approx. 3 large or 6 small**
- **2 tablespoons vegan butter melted**
- **2 tablespoons coconut sugar or brown sugar**
- **1 teaspoon cinnamon**
- **Nice cream**
- **Chopped walnuts or pecans**
- **Granola or oats gluten free if preferred**

INSTRUCTIONS

1. **Wash** and slice your peaches, and remove the pits. Put the sliced peaches in a small mixing dish and leave aside.
2. **Optional:** In another small bowl, combine the butter, sugar, and cinnamon. Then, pour the marinade over the cut peaches and mix thoroughly to coat them evenly. (If you want to eliminate extra fat and sugar, air fried the peaches without the mixture.)
3. **Place** the sliced peaches in a single layer in the air fryer basket and cook for 8-12 minutes at 350°F/177°C. They are ready when they are quite soft and a fork can easily puncture a peach slice.
4. **Serve** heated with desired toppings, or eat as is.

Tips:
- To get the finest flavor and natural sweetness, use ripe fresh peaches.
- Slice large peaches into six slices and tiny peaches into four slices.
- The ripeness of your peaches will impact the amount of time they cook. Riper/softer peaches cook faster than less ripe/harder ones.
- Remove any peach peels that have come loose when air frying.

Per Serving: Calories: 147cal; Carbohydrates: 23g; Protein: 1g; Sodium: 96mg; Potassium: 190mg; Fiber: 3g; Sugar: 18g; Calcium: 13mg; Iron: 1mg

FAST / FAMILY-FRIENDLY

MAKE	PREP TIME	COOK TIME	BAKE
6 puffs	20 mins	10 mins	320°F

INGREDIENTS

- **1 pound fresh ripe but firm peaches approx. 3 large or 6 small**
- **2 tablespoons vegan butter melted**
- **2 tablespoons coconut sugar or brown sugar**
- **1 teaspoon cinnamon**
- **Nice cream**
- **Chopped walnuts or pecans**
- **Granola or oats gluten free if preferred**

Apple Puffs with Vanilla Caramel Sauce

INSTRUCTIONS

1. **To** prepare the filling: In a bigger bowl, combine the apples, cinnamon, coconut sugar, and salt. Set aside.
2. **Spray** the air fryer basket with oil and put aside. Gently unroll the phyllo dough. Remove six pages and carefully set them aside. Wrap the remaining phyllo in sealed plastic wrap and place in the fridge.
3. **Remove** one large sheet of phyllo and place it on a clean, dry surface. Spray with oil. Fold it in thirds (long way, resulting in a long, thin rectangle). Spray each piece of dried phyllo as you go; this will produce a flaky (rather than dry) texture.
4. **Put** 1/3 cup apple mixture in the bottom of the phyllo rectangle. Fold the bottom of the phyllo up over the filling. Continue folding up to the top, creating a triangle as you go. After forming an apple-filled triangle, place it in the air fryer basket and brush the top with oil.
5. **Repeat** with the remaining phyllo and apple mixture. You'll probably only be able to fit three puffs in your air fryer at a time because you don't want them to overlap.
6. **Bake** for 10 minutes, or until very golden brown.

7. **To** pry the vanilla bean open, make a lengthwise cut along it with a sharp knife. Scrape out the insides with a table knife, then transfer to a small pot. Cook the maple syrup, oil, coconut sugar, and salt in a pot over medium-low heat, stirring until thoroughly blended. When the sauce boils, reduce to a moderate heat and simmer for 3 to 5 minutes, or until slightly thickened.

8. **Place** the apple puffs on a platter and cover with caramel sauce. Enjoy while warm.

Tips:
- Don't be hesitant to use phyllo (also known as filo) dough. There are only a few things to know. First, let frozen packets to thaw in the refrigerator overnight. I don't think it's necessary to cover the unwrapped dough with moist cloths, as most recipes suggest—just have the filling ready and work quickly once you've opened the box.

Per Serving: Calories: 366; Total fat: 16g; Saturated fat: 12g; Cholesterol: 0mg; Sodium: 296mg; Carbohydrates: 58g; Fiber: 3g; Protein: 2g

6
Staples

FAST / FAMILY-FRIENDLY / GLUTEN-FREE

SERVE
8

PREP TIME
5
mins

Non Dairy Ranch Dressing

INGREDIENTS

- 1 cup prepared vegan mayonnaise, your choice
- 4 teaspoons apple cider vinegar
- 4 teaspoons minced fresh parsley (or 1 tablespoon dried parsley)
- 4 small to medium garlic cloves, pressed or finely minced
- 1 teaspoon onion granules
- ½ teaspoon sea salt

INSTRUCTIONS

1. **In** a container, combine the mayonnaise, vinegar, parsley, garlic, onion, and salt; cover firmly and shake vigorously until well incorporated. If you're feeling very sophisticated, you can combine the ingredients in a bowl.

Tips:
- If the dressing is too thick, add up to 2 teaspoons of water until the required consistency is achieved. (I've discovered that it actually depends on the type of vegan mayonnaise you use.) This will keep refrigerated in an airtight jar for at least a week.

Per Serving: Calories: 76; Total fat: 7g; Saturated fat: 0g; Cholesterol: 0mg; Sodium: 258mg; Carbohydrates: 3g; Fiber: 0g; Protein: 1g

Asian Spicy Sweet Sauce

FAST / FAMILY-FRIENDLY / GLUTEN-FREE

MAKE 1 cup | PREP TIME 5 mins | COOK TIME 5 mins

INGREDIENTS

- 2 teaspoons arrowroot (or cornstarch)
- ½ cup water, divided
- ¼ cup tamari or shoyu
- ¼ cup agave nectar
- 1 tablespoon toasted sesame oil
- 4 large garlic cloves, minced or pressed
- ¼ to ½ teaspoon red chili flakes (adjust according to your heat preference)

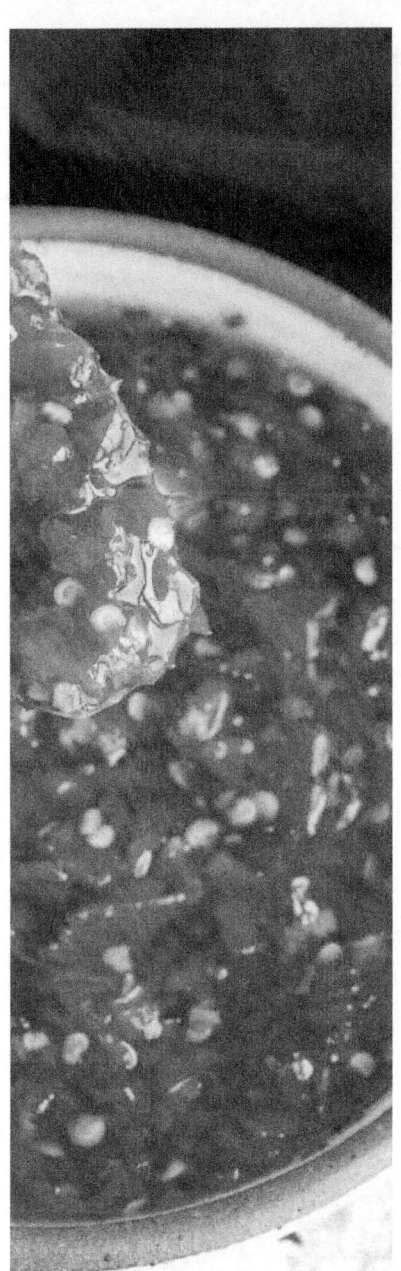

INSTRUCTIONS

1. **In** a medium saucepan, combine the arrowroot and 1 tablespoon water and whisk until dissolved.
2. **Add** the remaining water, tamari, agave, sesame oil, garlic, and chili flakes, and whisk over medium heat. Continue to cook, whisking often, until thicker in consistency.
3. **Remove** from heat once faintly thickened. This will keep refrigerated in an airtight jar for at least two weeks.

Per Serving (2 tablespoons): Calories: 80; Total fat: 2g; Saturated fat: 0g; Cholesterol: 0mg; Sodium: 0mg; Carbohydrates: 17g; Fiber: 1g; Protein: 0g

Cheesy Sauce

FAST / FAMILY-FRIENDLY / GLUTEN-FREE

MAKE
3
cup Dry Mix

PREP TIME
10
mins

COOK TIME
5
mins

INGREDIENTS

- **1 cup raw cashew pieces**
- **1¼ cups nutritional yeast**
- **½ cup rolled oats**
- **¼ cup arrowroot (or cornstarch)**
- **2 tablespoons seasoned salt**
- **2 tablespoons garlic granules**
- **1½ tablespoons onion granules**
- **½ teaspoon ground turmeric**
- **1 cup Dry Cheesy Mix**
- **¼ cup grated carrots**
- **¼ cup roasted red peppers (the jarred variety is fine)**
- **2 cups water, divided**

INSTRUCTIONS

1. **To** prepare the Dry Cheesy Mix: In a food processor, combine the cashews, nutritional yeast, oats, arrowroot, salt, garlic and onion granules, and turmeric. Blend until finely powdered. This dry mix can now be stored in the refrigerator (in an airtight container) for several months.
2. **In** a blender jar, combine the Dry Cheesy Mix, carrots, red pepper, and 1 cup water. Blend until smooth. Add the remaining 1 cup water and mix until very smooth.
3. **To** thicken, cook in a small pot over medium heat. Cook, whisking often, until thickened (should take less than 2 minutes). Serve warm.

Tips:

- When you know you'll be making a lot of cheesy sauce over the week, combine the dry mix, carrots, red pepper, and water. This liquid mixture can be refrigerated for up to a week before being whisked into a thick sauce on the stove in less than a minute.

Per Serving (¼ cup): Calories: 21; Total fat: 1g; Saturated fat: 0g; Cholesterol: 0mg; Sodium: 76mg; Carbohydrates: 4g; Fiber: 0g; Protein: 1g

Vegan BBQ Sauce

FAST / FAMILY-FRIENDLY / GLUTEN-FREE

SERVE
12

PREP TIME
5
mins

INGREDIENTS

- 1 cup no sugar added ketchup
- ¼ cup maple syrup
- 2 tablespoons apple cider vinegar
- 2 tablespoons low sodium Tamari or soy sauce if not avoiding gluten
- 1 teaspoon sriracha
- 1 teaspoon yellow mustard
- 1 teaspoon onion powder
- 1 teaspoon smoked paprika

INSTRUCTIONS

1. **Add** all of the ingredients to a small mixing bowl and whisk until well combined.
2. **Transfer** the BBQ sauce to a clean jar or container.

Tips:
- If you don't have or can't obtain sugar-free ketchup, use less maple syrup.
- Adjust to your preferences! If you prefer a spicier BBQ sauce, increase the hot sauce. Omit it if you want no heat.
- For an extra smokey flavor, add a teaspoon of liquid smoke or double the smoked paprika.
- Refrigerate the sauce in a sealed jar or container for up to three weeks. Alternatively, freeze tightly for up to three months.

Per Serving (approx. 2 tablespoons): Calories: 34cal; Carbohydrates: 6g; Sodium: 293mg; Potassium: 33mg; Sugar: 5g; Calcium: 10mg

Cilantro Chutney

FAST / GLUTEN-FREE

MAKE
1½
cups

PREP TIME
10
mins

INGREDIENTS

- **1 cup fresh cilantro**
- **⅓ cup finely shredded unsweetened coconut**
- **2 tablespoons chopped fresh ginger**
- **3 medium garlic cloves, peeled**
- **½ jalapeño, seeds removed**
- **1 teaspoon cumin seeds**
- **½ teaspoon sea salt**
- **2 tablespoons fresh lime juice**
- **½ cup water**

INSTRUCTIONS

1. **In** a food processor or blender, combine cilantro, coconut, ginger, garlic, and jalapeño. Blend thoroughly, but the mixture should not be completely smooth.
2. **Blend** in the cumin, salt, lime juice, and water until well blended, but with a little texture left. Serve cold or room temperature. When stored in an airtight container, this will stay in the fridge for a week or two.

Per Serving (2 tablespoons): Calories: 21; Total fat: 2g; Saturated fat: 1g; Cholesterol: 0mg; Sodium: 80mg; Carbohydrates: 2g; Fiber: 1g; Protein: 0g

Crisp Tofu

FAST / FAMILY-FRIENDLY / GLUTEN-FREE

SERVE	PREP TIME	COOK TIME	FRY
3	2 mins	16 mins	392°F

INGREDIENTS

- **1 package (8 ounces) of firm or extra-firm tofu**
- **2 tablespoons of neutral-flavored oil (such refined coconut, sunflower, or safflower), split**
- **Cooking oil spray (sunflower, safflower, or refined coconut).**
- **1/4 teaspoon sea salt**

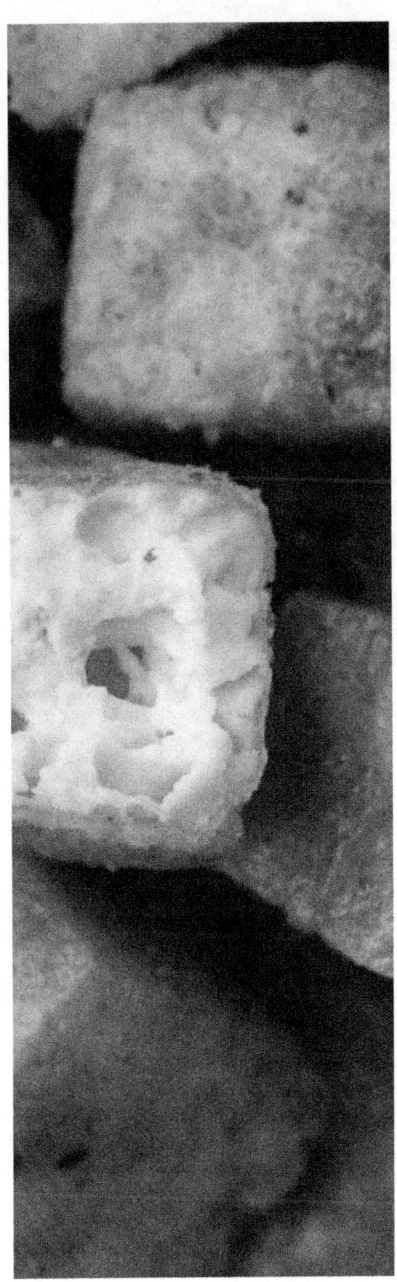

INSTRUCTIONS

1. **For** this dish, cut the tofu into 1/2-inch thick slabs without pressing it. Next, cut the slabs into triangles about an inch in size.
2. **In** a medium bowl, gently toss the tofu with 1 teaspoon oil. Spray oil on your air fryer basket. Place the tofu in the air fryer basket and cook for 8 minutes. Set aside the bowl for later use.
3. **To** fully coat the tofu, gently toss it in the remaining oil and salt using a rubber spatula. Place the tofu back in the air fryer basket and cook for 8 minutes, or until golden brown and crispy. Enjoy while warm.

Tips:
- When selecting tofu for any savory application, you should look for a water-packed firm or extra-firm variety. Keep in mind that silken tofu has a totally distinct texture, making it suitable for smooth-textured sweets like the cream sauce in the Strawberry Delight Breakfast Parfait but not for most savory dishes. Silken tofu is offered in aseptic packs and is not refrigerated, as opposed to the water-packed, refrigerated version that I use in this recipe.

Per Serving: Calories: 81; Total fat: 6g; Saturated fat: 1g; Cholesterol: 0mg; Sodium: 165mg; Carbohydrates: 1g; Fiber: 1g; Protein: 6g

Sesame Crunch Tofu

FAST / FAMILY-FRIENDLY / GLUTEN-FREE

SERVE	PREP TIME	COOK TIME	BAKE
3	10 mins	20 mins	392°F

INGREDIENTS

- **1 package (8 ounces) of firm or extra-firm tofu**
- **1 1/2 teaspoons tamari or shoyu**
- **1/2 teaspoon granulated garlic.**
- **1/3 cup raw sesame seeds (untoasted)**
- **2 teaspoons flour (whole-wheat pastry, chickpeas, brown rice)**
- **1 tablespoon arrowroot (or cornstarch).**
- **2 tablespoons of neutral-flavored oil (such as sunflower, safflower, or refined coconut).**
- **Cooking oil spray (sunflower, safflower, or refined coconut).**

INSTRUCTIONS

1. **Cut** the tofu into 1/2-inch thick slabs, then triangles.
2. **To** press the tofu, place it in a single layer on paper towels or a tea towel and cover with more towels. To remove extra moisture, press down softly but firmly.
3. **Place** the pressed tofu onto a platter. Sprinkle the tamari and garlic evenly. Turn to ensure proper coating.
4. **In** a medium mixing dish, add sesame seeds, flour, and arrowroot. Add the tofu and stir gently with a rubber spatula until uniformly coated with the sesame mixture. Finally, add the oil and toss to coat the tofu.
5. **Spray** oil in your air fryer basket. Place the tofu in a single layer in the air fryer basket and bake for 10 minutes. Remove. Turn the pieces over and cook for another 10 minutes, or until golden brown and crisp. Remove and enjoy.

Per Serving: Calories: 183; Total fat: 18g; Saturated fat: 2g; Cholesterol: 0mg; Sodium: 505mg; Carbohydrates: 5g; Fiber: 2g; Protein: 4g

Green Chili Sauce

FAST / GLUTEN-FREE

MAKE
2
cups

PREP TIME
5
mins

COOK TIME
5
mins

INGREDIENTS

- **1 teaspoon of neutral-flavored oil (sunflower, safflower, or refined coconut).**
- **1 tablespoon flour (brown rice or chickpeas)**
- **1 (13-ounce) container (about. 1½ cups). roasted, peeled, chopped green chiles, thawed (if frozen)**
- **2 teaspoons of coconut sugar.**
- **1/4 cup plus 1 teaspoon fresh lime juice.**
- **1 1/4 tsp sea salt 5 medium garlic cloves, chopped or pressed.**

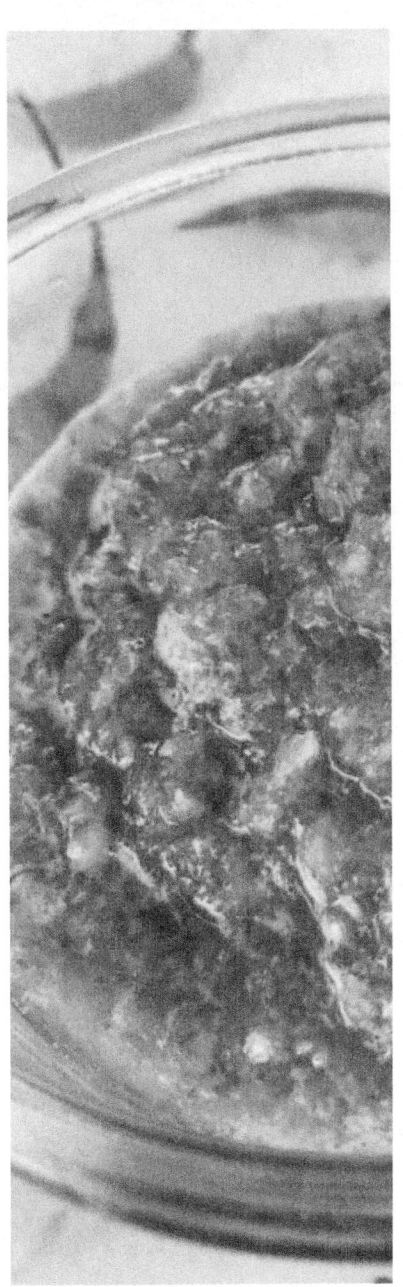

INSTRUCTIONS

1. **In** a medium saucepan, combine the oil and flour, stirring until smooth. Add the green chiles and coconut sugar, and simmer for 5 minutes, stirring frequently, until the mixture thickens.
2. **Turn** off the heat and add the lime juice, sea salt, and garlic. Mix well and serve. This will keep refrigerated in an airtight jar for approximately a week.

Tips:
- If you prefer a really thick sauce, add a little more flour until the required consistency is achieved. Even if you enjoy spicy meals, you may prefer mild green chiles (rather than medium or hot). Even mild green chiles may be very hot, and if you're like me and like to consume a bit too much of this sauce at once, the heat may be too intense.

Per Serving (¼ cup): Calories: 21; Total fat: 1g; Saturated fat: 0g; Cholesterol: 0mg; Sodium: 76mg; Carbohydrates: 4g; Fiber: 0g; Protein: 1g

THANK YOU FOR READING

Printed in Great Britain
by Amazon